Amazon Echo Dot User Manual: Guide to Unleash your Wireless Speaker Device!

By Shelby Johnson

www.techmediasource.com

Disclaimer:

This eBook is an unofficial guide for using the Amazon Echo Dot product and is not meant to replace any official documentation that came with the device or accessories. The information in this guide is meant as recommendations and suggestions, but the author bears no responsibility for any issues arising from improper use of the Amazon Echo Dot. The owner of the device is responsible for taking all necessary precautions and measures with their device.

Amazon Echo and Echo Dot are trademarks of Amazon and/or its affiliates. All other trademarks are the property of their respective owners. The author and publishers of this book are not associated with any product or vendor mentioned in this book. Any Amazon Echo Dot screenshots are meant for educational purposes only.

Contents

Contents 5

Introduction 9

Amazon Echo vs. Echo Dot vs. Tap 11

What's in the Echo Dot Box? 13

Getting Started 15

   To Connect to Wi-Fi 15

      Alexa or Echo App 16

   Echo Dot's Buttons, Controls & Lights 17

Using Echo Dot for Information 19

   Weather Requests 19

   Traffic Requests 20

   Wikipedia and Fun Fact Requests 20

   Joke Requests 22

   Team Scores and Game Time Requests 22

Using Alexa App & Web Settings 23

   To-do List & Shopping List 23

   Set a Timer or Alarm 24

      Set a Timer 25

      Set an Alarm 26

      Alarm and Timer IFTTT 26

   Settings 27

   Set up a New Echo, Tap or Dot 30

   History 30

   Music & Media 31

   Flash Briefing 32

Sports Update 32

Traffic 32

Calendar 33

Lists 33

Voice Purchasing 33

Household profile 34

About the Amazon Alexa app 34

Using Your Echo Dot Remotely or on the Go 34

New Updates & Software Development 35

Tips and Tricks for Amazon Echo Dot 37

How to Complete a Voice Training Lesson for Echo Dot 37

How to Listen to Music 38

How to Play Prime Music through Echo Dot 39

Amazon Music Unlimited 40

How to Connect iHeartRadio to Echo Dot 41

How to Listen to TuneIn Radio 42

How to Listen to Pandora 42

How to Listen to Spotify 44

How to Buy Music 45

Music Controls 45

Stream Music from iTunes, Spotify, or others using Pairing Tap with Devices 47

How to Create To Do Lists, Shopping Lists and More 48

How to use Echo Dot with Google Calendar 49

How to use the Skills Features on Echo Dot 50

How to order a Pizza or Uber on the Dot 51

Ten Cool Skills to Try on Dot 52

Echo Dot Accessories 57

Using Dot with Compatible Smart Home Devices 61

Creating a Smart Home Group of Devices 62

Some Quick Dot Q&A's 65

Do I need an Amazon Echo or Tap to have the Dot? 65

Do I need an Amazon Prime membership for the Dot to work? 65

Can I have a Dot, Echo, and a Tap all together in my home or other area? 66

Can I put a Dot in different floors and/or rooms of my home? 66

Do all Dot devices in my home (or other environment) need to be connected to the same Amazon account? 66

Can I bring Dot from my home on a trip or to an office, etc.? 67

Is the Dot able to be portable in my home or other area, so I can move it around and use it without it being plugged in? 67

Get Help with Issues or Provide Feedback 69

Conclusion 71

Other guides by Shelby Johnson 73

Introduction

Amazon's new Echo Dot is a fun and helpful new device that allows you to use the Alexa interactive voice service and related features in your home, office or any other environment that you choose to set it up in. Alexa (or Echo if you change the wake word), is the ultimate household personal assistant, allowing for you to do all sorts of tasks. Alexa is the remote, your computer, and your mobile devices. Alexa will play music, give you news, weather or sports updates, order you a pizza or Uber, tell you jokes, and even help you control lights or other smart home devices. And those are just a few of the many features!

The Dot wireless speaker seems compact and basic, but don't be fooled by its size as it offers a lot of great features. At first, it might seem overwhelming to unlock all the awesome features the Dot has to offer, but this unofficial user manual is here to help guide you through the setup and beyond. Together we can unleash the power of the new Amazon Echo Dot!

Amazon Echo vs. Echo Dot vs. Tap

For those wondering, the Amazon Echo products carry many similarities but are also quite different. The Echo was the first iteration of Amazon's interactive full-sized speaker featuring Alexa voice technology and was first introduced to only Amazon Prime members. It can be accessed simply by speaking "Alexa," followed by a command or request. There is no touching the device required, unless one wants to use the button on it or turn the top to adjust volume. It also is plugged into the wall at all times.

The Echo Dot is basically a smaller version of the Echo. It also is hands-free with voice commands used to wake it and perform various tasks. The Dot also must stay plugged into the wall (power outlet) at all times. Where it differs most is by its size, and by the fact that users must plug it into a stereo or compatible speaker in order to really enjoy its sound.

The Tap is the other speaker from Amazon which is much more portable. It also features voice interactive commands and requests with Alexa, but you will need to press the microphone button on the Tap to make your requests. Basically, Tap is not always listening, whereas the Echo is. However, the Tap is smaller and lighter, making it highly portable. It also doesn't need to be constantly plugged in for its use.

You can do a variety of tasks using the Echo, Dot, or Tap which include but aren't limited to: getting weather or sports information, setting timers or alarms, setting up or checking "To Do" and shopping lists, ordering items from Amazon, listening to music from your library or the Amazon Prime library (if you're a member) and utilizing various "Skills" which are helpful features that you can enable in the Alexa app.

Skills that you can set include everything from playing a daily "Jeopardy" game to ordering an Uber, checking on flight prices or ordering a pizza. You also can use the Echo, Dot or Tap to connect with various compatible home automation devices for convenient control of various household items. Basically, these devices are constantly evolving and full of great uses!

What's in the Echo Dot Box?

When you open the new Amazon Echo Dot box, you are going to recognize everything inside as standard electronic devices and their necessary counterparts for operation. That is to say, nothing is going to jump out and spin in circles welcoming you to a new world of wireless interactive speakers, although there are a lot of things in store with the latest streaming device. Inside you will find:

- Echo Dot speaker device
- MicroUSB Power Cord
- USB wall charger brick
- Charging Cradle
- Quick Start Guide & Things to Try

Getting Started

To get started with the Amazon Echo Dot, complete the following steps:

1. Unpack the device and related items from the box.
2. Plug the power cord into the charging cradle and then into an electrical outlet.
3. Download the Alexa app to your mobile device or use your computer for setup from www.amazon.com/alexasetup.

Once you plug in the charger, the Echo Dot will start charging. After about a bit, Alexa will greet you, and you are ready for the device's initial setup. The Alexa/Echo app or website will help walk you through the setup process.

To Connect to Wi-Fi

- Go to Alexa app.
- Connect to Amazon-xxx Wi-Fi Network.
- Press continue.
- Select your Wi-Fi network, and wait while your Echo Dot prepares to connect. (Note: you may need to press the Bluetooth/Wireless button on back of your Echo Dot to make sure it connects)
- Once the Echo Dot is connected, go back to your computer's Wi-Fi connection and reconnect your computer to your Wi-Fi network.
- Watch video on Amazon Echo Dot.

Note: *If you use multiple mobile devices and your computer, you can download the app to each device, so you will always have access to Alexa. Simply complete the setup on one device and then download the app on all of your other devices.*

Once Alexa is connected to your computer, you will be able to login to your Wi-Fi network using your computer (or with your mobile device if you downloaded the app). To do this, make sure to choose your Wi-Fi from the list you see, and type in your password, if necessary.

Next, go back to your computer Wi-Fi settings, and choose your network to allow your computer to reconnect to your Wi-Fi network in order to finish setting up your Echo Dot.

Once you see that the Wi-Fi is connected, click "Continue."

Alexa or Echo App

The Alexa or Echo app is available on the following mobile devices:

- Fire tablets and phones via Amazon app (running Fire OS 2.0 or above)
- Android phones and tablets via Google Play (running Android 4.0 or above)
- iOS phones and tablets via iTunes App Store (running iOS 7.0 or above)

You can also use the Echo App via http://echo.amazon.com on the following web browsers on your computer:

- Safari
- Chrome
- Firefox
- Internet Explorer (10 or above)

Echo Dot's Buttons, Controls & Lights

As of this publication, the newest version of the Echo Dot device has a variety of buttons, outputs, and different colored lights you'll want to be familiar with in order to use it.

On the back side of the device you'll see an input and an output connection area. On one side is the microUSB cable output for connecting your Dot to a power source. Next to that is a 3.5 mm audio cable to for outputting music to a speaker or stereo system.

On the very top of the device are four buttons (as seen in the image that follows). The plus and minus buttons will adjust the volume of your device up (+) or down (-). The microphone button with a line through the microphone will stop Alexa from being able to hear you. This is helpful if you are on the phone and don't want to inadvertently say the trigger word "Alexa" and have the device responding. To reactivate voice response, simply press the microphone button again. Finally, on the opposite side of that button is a button with a small dot in it. Press this if you want to activate your Dot to make a request without speaking first to wake it up.

The ring of lights that go around the top of your Dot are important to pay attention to. Blue lights are generally when your Dot is working or you're making a request. A red light will usually indicate that your device is having difficulty connecting to your wireless network. Other light colors you may see include orange when first trying to set up the device on a wireless network.

Using Echo Dot for Information

One of the most useful features of the Amazon Echo Dot is its ability to retrieve information upon request. For the most part, the information will be obtained from Bing or Wikipedia listings, as of this guide's initial publication.

Weather Requests

The most basic request to make is asking about the weather. Simply ask out loud, "What's the weather?" or "What's the temperature?" and you will get the current temperature and day's forecast for the location you are in (or the zip code you have set for your location within your Echo app).

You can also ask "What is tomorrow's forecast?" or "What is the weekend forecast?" to get future weather information.

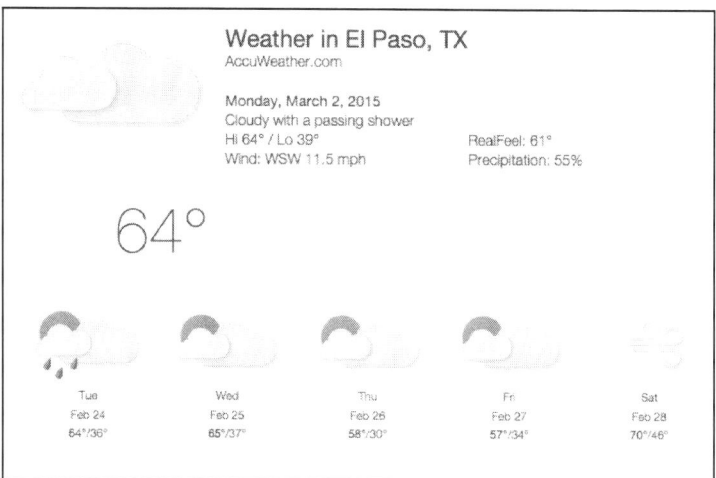

Finally, you can ask, "Alexa, what is the weather in (name of place)?" to get the weather information on any other place in the world you may want to know about.

Note: *You can say "Alexa stop" when it is telling you weather information, or "Alexa cancel" to stop the weather info playback.*

Traffic Requests

You can find out about traffic conditions using the Amazon Echo Dot. To do this complete the following steps:

1. Enter your starting point and destination in the Alexa App.
2. Press the microphone and ask a question about the traffic on your route. For example, you can ask, "Alexa, how is traffic?"

Wikipedia and Fun Fact Requests

You can ask "When is Father's Day?" for example and Alexa will tell you the date in the current year that the holiday falls on.

You could also ask Alexa who wrote a certain book, a definition of a word, a fun fact such as the size of a monument, a celebrity, politician or athlete's age (or date of birth) or for a measurement conversion.

To get more detailed information on many topics you can simply say "Alexa, Wikipedia George Washington," for example. Alexa will begin speaking important information to you about the requested topic, as obtained from Wikipedia.

Note: *You can always go into your Echo app or the Echo web portal for your Amazon account to your Home area to see a history of your requests. With some of the requests you can also get even more information online about the various topics you received info for by clicking on the "Search Bing for (requested info)" option.*

Every so often, Amazon unveils a special interactive feature to use with your Echo Dot or Echo. At one point, there was a feature to celebrate Dr. Seuss's birthday. You could use the following questions or voice prompts to explore this feature:

- "Alexa, do you like green eggs and ham?"
- "Alexa, one fish, two fish."
- "Alexa, why do you sit there like that?"
- "Alexa, what was the Lorax?"

You can also receive Star Trek wisdom from your Echo Dot by simply saying "Alexa, live long and prosper." Other features are released by Amazon with special events such as the Oscars or other awards shows, March Madness college basketball and the U.S. Presidential Election.

Joke Requests

If you need a quick laugh, simply ask "Alexa, tell me a joke" for the Echo Dot to give you one of many jokes it has stored in its database! The Echo Dot is quite adept at knock knock jokes, so be sure to ask it a few. Simply press the microphone button and say "Alexa, knock knock" and see what Alexa comes up with.

Another fun joke to ask Alexa is "Alexa, why did the chicken cross the road?" The answer varies each time, and it can be quite humorous.

Team Scores and Game Time Requests

You can use your Echo Dot to stay up-to-date with your favorite sports teams. Not only will Alexa tell you the results of a team's most recent game, but it will also tell you information about the team's next game including opponent, date, and game time.

Currently, Alexa provides scores for NBA, WNBA, NHL, NCAA, NFL, MLB, and MLS games. You can ask for scores and schedule information for teams from these professional leagues. For example, you can ask, "Alexa, who won the Chicago Bulls game?" or "Alexa when do the New York Rangers play?" and you will receive information on the sports team you asked about.

You can also ask "Alexa, what's the score of the Duke Blue Devils game?" and receive a live score if that particular team has a game in progress.

To find out information about your favorite team simply ask "Alexa, when is the next "Team Name" game. Alexa will respond with the information.

Using Alexa App & Web Settings

While the Echo Dot itself is voice controlled, you can also do a lot of things via the Alexa app or http://echo.amazon.com website account settings.

To-do List & Shopping List

In this area of your app or Echo web account, you can add items to your to-do or shopping lists. To do so, simply tap or click on either list. Type the new item into the box that says "Add item."

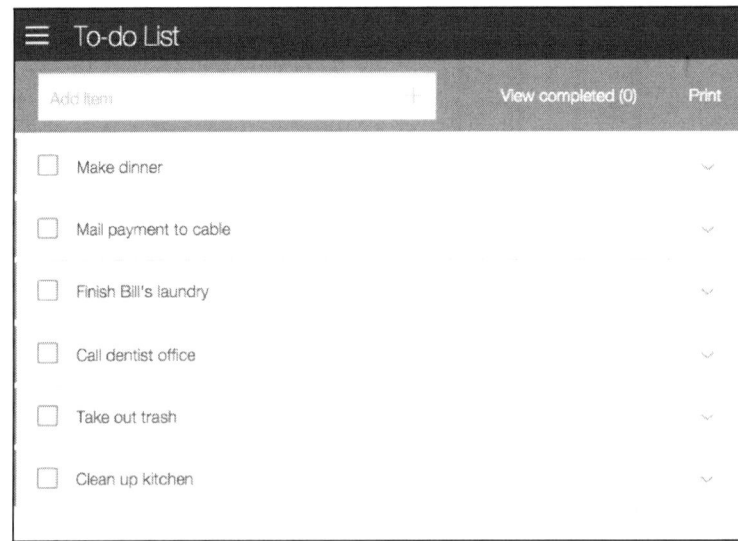

You can also check off completed items on the list by clicking or tapping on the check box next to them. Additionally, you can go over to the right of any item and click on the dropdown area. This will give you options to move the item to your other list, or Delete item from your list.

One other great option you have with your lists is the "Print" option, which is located in the upper right hand corner. Use this to print out a shopping list when you're heading to the store, making it extra convenient! Of course, if you would rather not print out the list, it will be available right on the Alexa app on your mobile device.

Keep in mind, that items you add manually should be spoken back to you when you ask your Echo Dot what's on your To-do or Shopping list, but how well it speaks each item may depend on how much voice training you have done with the device.

Tip: *If something on your To-do list was transcribed wrong onto the list, you can tap or click on the item from the Alexa app, and hear a recording of your voice as you said it.*

Set a Timer or Alarm

You can use your Echo Dot as a way to time something you are doing, or to set a gentle but helpful alarm. This is especially useful if you are timing how long you are cooking something for and don't want to tie up a stove or microwave timer/alarm.

Set a Timer

To set the timer for a certain set amount of time, you can press the microphone button, speak to the Echo Dot and say "Alexa, set a timer for 15 minutes," for example. You can also set a timer with the Alexa app or via the web portal.

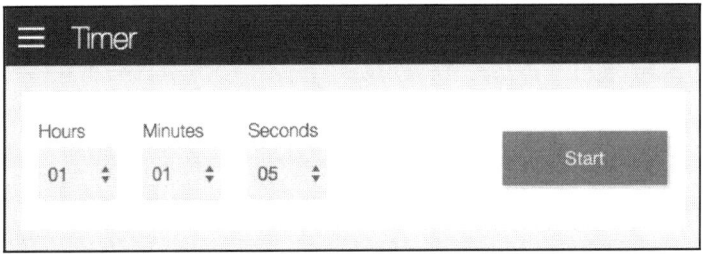

1. Click or tap on the "Timer" option on the left side options.
2. Adjust the Hours, Minutes and Seconds to the amount of time you want to countdown from.
3. Click or tap on the "Start" button at the far right to begin the timer.
4. At any time while the timer is counting down, you can tap or click on "Cancel" to cancel the timer, or tap or click on "Pause" to pause it for a moment.
5. Once the timer has completed its countdown, the Echo will give a series of sounds to let you know. You can use the app or web portal to tap or click on "Cancel" to stop the chirps. Alternately, you can say "Alexa, stop" to stop the chirping.

Set an Alarm

You can also set up an alarm to sound at a certain time. You can speak to the Echo and say "Alexa, set an alarm from 5:30 p.m." for example. You can also set an alarm inside the Alexa app or web portal.

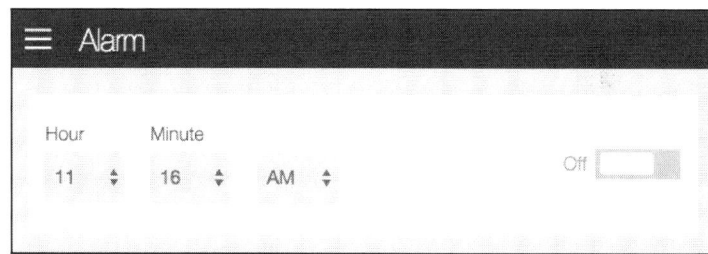

1. Click or tap on the "Alarm" option on your left side options.
2. Adjust the hour and minute as well as AM or PM.
3. Move the slider to On, if it is Off.
4. The Echo Dot will now function as a daily alarm clock for this time. It will make a gentle but noticeable series of chirping beeps, which are different than the timer sound. Say "Alexa, stop" to stop the alarm from sounding.
5. You can go back into the Alarm settings are and move the slider to "Off" when you no longer want the alarm to continue each day.

Alarm and Timer IFTTT

IFTTT stands for "If This, Then That." This unique service connects your favorite devices, apps, and websites with simple "recipes," which are sets of rules. The Echo has the ability to trigger IFTTT actions when an alarm goes off or when a timer you set has ended.

For example: If you want to turn the lights on when your alarm goes off, IF you asked Alexa to set an alarm to wake up, THEN your lights can be turned on when that alarm goes off.

To activate IFTTT for your Echo Dot device, sign up here https://ifttt.com/. Once you have signed up, you need to activate the Amazon Alexa channel. After you've linked your IFTTT account with your Echo Dot, you can use some of the shared recipes to get started with the IFTTT functionality of the Echo Dot. This particular feature can also be helpful with many smart home tasks, if needed.

Settings

In this section, you can modify various settings related to your Amazon Echo Dot. To do so, tap or click on the "Settings" option on the left side menu of your app or Echo web portal.

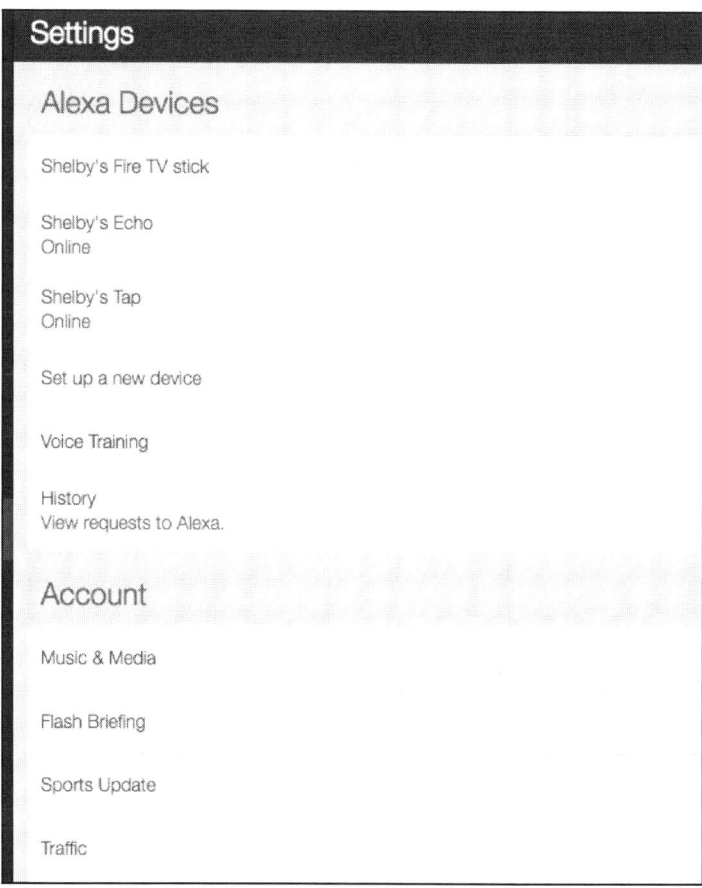

These include the following:

- **Your device name (if it's on or offline)** - by tapping or clicking on this setting, you can bring up a variety of settings to adjust or other information about your device, including:
- **Update the Wi-Fi settings** – Use this to adjust the Wi-Fi network you are connected to.
- **Bluetooth** - enter pairing mode or clear all paired Bluetooth devices
- **Echo remote** - it may say connected, and you can click on "Forget remote" if you want to unpair it.

- **Echo device name -** Tap or click on this setting and you can modify the name of your Echo, i.e. "Mom's Echo" or "Jim's Echo," etc.
- **Echo device location -** you can set your specific zip code to help get localized weather information, alarms and flash briefings.
- **Wake word -** This is the word or name you speak before your requests to the Echo. As of this publication, Echo has two wake words. The standard it is set to is "Alexa." If you desire, you can change the wake word to "Amazon." Remember, if you change it to "Amazon," you will need to say that before each request you make.
- **Metric measurements -** You can move the slider to ON to use metric measurements for temperature and distance.
- **Sounds -** By tapping or clicking on this setting, you can adjust the alarm and timer volume, or choose to have a sound play after you wake the Echo and after you finish speaking to your Echo.
- **Echo is registered to -** It should have the name of the device owner here as it is connected to their Amazon account. If you transfer ownership, you can deregister the Echo from its current Amazon account with this setting.
- **Echo software version -** This will tell you that you have the latest updated version of the software. Echo does automatic online updates as new features and software are released.
- **Serial number -** This is important to note should you have to do any tech troubleshooting with Amazon for your device.

Set up a New Echo, Tap or Dot

You can tap or click on this option if you need to set up a new Echo, Tap or Dot device in your home, office or other environment.

History

You can tap or click on this option to see your various voice interactions and requested information from the Echo. You can click on any specific request there to see more details about it, listen to a recorded playback of your request, provide feedback (did the device hear you correctly?) and also delete recordings of your voice request.

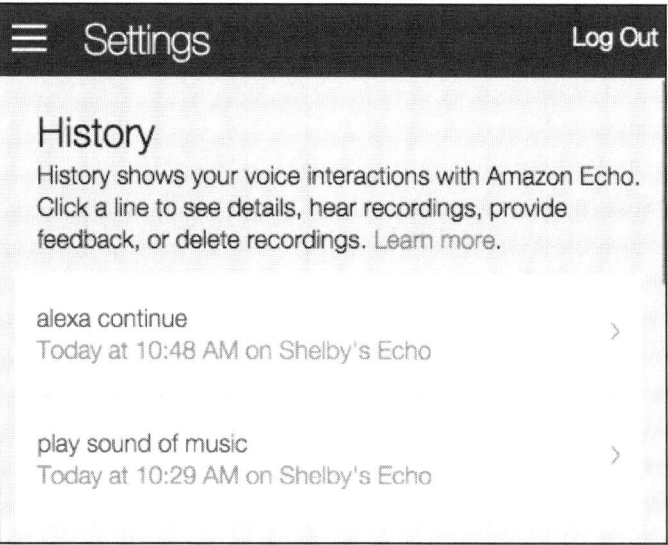

Music & Media

You can tap or click on this option to adjust accounts for Amazon Music, iHeartRadio, Spotify, Pandora and TuneIn, among others. In particular, you can use this area to connect your compatible music accounts if you have one, set up your default music streaming services for the Dot, or simply adjust individual settings for the services such as the following for iHeartRadio:

- *"Enable custom stations"* will enable or disable iHeartRadio's creation of custom stations based on your listening preferences. You can move the slider to "On" to get custom radio stations or to "Off" to disable them. Keep in mind some of the custom radio stations may have content that is inappropriate for those listeners who are under the age of 13.
- *"Broadcast to Facebook"* will associate iHeartRadio with your Facebook account so it will share your iHeartRadio activity (songs or stations played, etc.) on your Facebook timeline. Use the slider here to set this "On" or "Off" based on your preference.
- *"Manage iHeartRadio settings"* will help you go to the iHeart.com website and adjust your settings even more, or to learn more about the terms of conditions for using iHeartRadio.

Flash Briefing

You can tap or click on this option to customize the type of flash briefing news that you will hear read from text-to-speech from the Echo. For example, you can move sliders to "On" or "Off" for various headline news topics such as sports, business, politics, world, etc. You can also move sliders to "On" or "Off" for NPR News and BBC Radio. Additional briefing news is available for ABC Headline News, Good Morning America, Fox Sports, and Jimmy Kimmel Live the Morning After, all from iHeartRadio.

Sports Update

You can tap or click on this option to choose your favorite professional sports teams. Choose from teams by typing MLB, NFL, NHL, NBA and college team names into the search box and then select the ones you want to add. Next time you ask for a sports update from Alexa, you'll be given specific information pertaining to these teams, including their scores, schedules, and more.

Traffic

By tapping or clicking on this settings option you can set up a particular to and from you may travel frequently, such as a commute to work, or a drive to a relative or friend's home. By adding the "to" and "from" addresses, you can get detailed information from Alexa regarding the traffic on this route.

Calendar

Here is where you can link your Google account and Google calendar for use with Alexa. You will need to have a valid Google or Gmail account in order to do this, but once you do, you can use the calendar with Alexa. There's more on this feature later in this guide.

Lists

Tap or click on the Lists option and you can link two helpful productivity apps to your Alexa: Any.do and Todolist. If you want to increase your productivity or decrease your forgetfulness, this feature can be great to use with Alexa and your mobile devices for setting up lists to keep track of tasks, shopping items, and more!

Voice Purchasing

You can tap or click on this option to enable or disable "Purchase by voice." This setting basically allows you to purchase music you want from Amazon's digital music store.

You can also set up a 4-digit code to prevent other users from making unauthorized purchases through your Echo, a very helpful extra means of security.

Finally, in this particular settings area you can manage your 1-Click settings for whichever "1-Click payment method" you have set up in your Amazon account.

Household profile

You can tap or click on this option to invite other members of your household with separate Amazon accounts to access the Echo. This will set up joint shopping and to-do lists, allow for setting individual flash briefing preferences and also allow playback of the other household member's Amazon music on the Echo.

Follow on-screen instructions to set up an additional household profile.

Note: *An Amazon Household allows for 2 adults and 4 children among a shared household profile.*

About the Amazon Alexa app

You can tap or click on this particular menu option to see the host name and client version for your Echo app. This info can be helpful if you are trying to troubleshoot a technical problem with customer support, but it may not be needed.

Using Your Echo Dot Remotely or on the Go

You can use the Amazon Echo Dot device when you are away from your home, as long as the Echo Dot has power and is connected to an available Wi-Fi network. This can include connecting to a public hotspot, a friend or relative's Wi-Fi network, or if you have a Wi-Fi hotspot ability with your smart phone or other device. Simply go through the steps with your Alexa app to connect your device to the new network.

While you are away from home, as long as you have a compatible mobile device on a working wireless or cellular network, you should be able to open your Echo app. You can then perform certain requests inside the app such as playing back Amazon Music, a TuneIn station, or even setting a timer or alarm.

Alternately, you can use your Echo Dot as a portable speaker with the 3.5mm audio cable plugin or Bluetooth wireless technology and connect an audio device to listen to music or other audio.

New Updates& Software Development

As mentioned in this guide, the Echo Dot software should automatically update with new functions or features without needing to perform any additional actions. You will also receive email updates from Amazon as new features and voice commands are added to the device.

For example, shortly after the original Echo was released, it received the following updated voice requests:

3. "Alexa, play rock, scissors, paper" – Give this voice command and prepare your choice: rock, scissors, or paper. Alexa will tell you her choice to see who wins!
4. "Alexa, flip a coin" – Use this to settle who goes first. Alexa will give you heads or tail each time.
5. "Alexa, roll the dice" – Alexa will provide you with a random roll of the dice and give you the number it lands on!

It is very likely that more new voice commands, features and functions will continue to be added to the device in the future. As you'll find out in some of the sections that follow, new "Skills" and Smart home device compatibility is being added quite a bit!

Tips and Tricks for Amazon Echo Dot

The biggest tips to get the most out of your Echo Dot device are to make sure the voice recognition fully understands your requests and also to customize the various settings to your liking. The following sections will break down how to do that while also presenting some additional tips and suggestions.

How to Complete a Voice Training Lesson for Echo Dot

To help the Echo Dot understand your spoken requests better, you can perform voice-training sessions. These sessions consist of 25 different statements or requests that you will have to speak to the Echo Dot.

To perform voice training, complete the following steps:

1. Launch your Amazon Alexa app on your mobile device OR go to the http://echo.amazon.com with your Amazon login to access your Echo settings.
2. Click on or tap on the settings area of the app denoted by the three horizontal lines in the left-hand corner.
3. Scroll down to "Voice Training" and tap or click on it.
4. The Voice Training area of the app or site will launch with basic instructions on how to use it.

Note: *After you complete a voice training session, you can go back in and do another training at any time to further help the Echo Dot with recognizing your voice and requests.*

How to Listen to Music

The Echo Dot will allow you to listen to streaming music in many ways. If you're a Prime member, you have access to a variety of free streaming songs. If you're not an Amazon Prime member, you are able to listen to any digital songs you have purchased from Amazon in the past (or any songs you have uploaded to your Amazon music library). These songs are stored in your free Amazon cloud online on your account.

To play a song from your library complete the following steps:

1. Press the microphone button and say, "Alexa, play (song or artist name)."
2. If Alexa hears it correctly, it should begin to play the song you requested, or a random assortment of tracks from an album, artist, or playlist you requested.

Note: *If you ask Alexa to play a song you don't own, or it hears the song you asked for incorrectly, then it will likely play you a preview of a song you can purchase from Amazon instead. Say "Alexa, cancel" or "Alexa, stop" to try your spoken request again.*

How to Play Prime Music through Echo Dot

Playing music on the Echo Dot is easy to do, but offers much more if you are an Amazon Prime member. Prime members enjoy millions of free songs from a variety of genres, artists, playlists and more. All you need to do is ask "Alexa, Play Katy Perry," or "Barbara Streisand" or "John Legend" or whichever other artist you want to hear from the Prime free music catalog. If the requested song is available, the Dot will begin to stream that for you. You can also ask for a specific genre of music, such as pop, or rock, hip-hop, or classical, to receive a variety of songs.

There are over a million songs in the Prime database, from Daft Punk to Bruce Springsteen, and more music is being added all the time. You can fill your library with Prime Music and find the best music from your favorite artists or even follow Amazon's personalized recommendations to discover new music and your next favorite artist.

You can take advantage of hundreds of Prime Playlists created for you when you want to listen to music but don't want to hover over the list of available music selecting every song. You can even find Playlists that are relevant to what you want to hear, how you're feeling, the best genre, and the artist you really love listening to. Amazon Prime Music does the work for you.

You can also create your own playlists in Prime Music, give them a name, and then ask Alexa to play a specific playlist. To create Prime Music playlists, complete the following steps from your Amazon music library either on the web or inside an app:

- Click the check boxes next to the songs you want to add to the playlist.
- Click Add to playlist.

- Click New playlist from the drop-down list to create a new playlist. You will create a name for the playlist.
- When you want to play a specific playlist on the Echo Dot say, "Alexa play playlist 'x' and the Echo Dot will play that playlist.

Note: *If you ask Alexa to play a song that is not available for free to Prime members, you will likely get a preview of the track, with the opportunity to purchase it after it previews.*

Amazon Music Unlimited

Amazon Music Unlimited is a monthly service that Amazon released in 2016 for those who want to unlock even more streaming music beyond what Prime Music offers. Basically, the Amazon Music Unlimited service allows subscribers to unlock tens of millions of songs to stream on the Dot, Echo or Tap devices. In addition, the service offers unique voice commands such as "Alexa, play the song with the lyrics (insert your lyrics of choice)," or "Alexa, play the song of the day," or "Alexa, play happy pop music."

As of this publication, Prime members could get the Amazon Music Unlimited service for the price of $7.99 a month, while non-Prime members would need to pay $9.99 a month. There is also a single-device plan for $3.99 and a monthly family plan for $14.99 available. These various plans were also made available for purchase on an annual rate which is less expensive overall.

Note: *The Amazon Music Unlimited service is not necessary in order to enjoy music on your device but is a way to enhance or add more music options.*

How to Connect iHeartRadio to Echo Dot

This Clear Channel owned radio station provides aggregated radio content from over 800 different radio stations, making the culmination of content available to users. The content is completely free to enjoy, making for a great listening experience on your Echo Dot with this online radio and music app.

To connect your iHeartRadio to Echo Dot, complete the following steps:

1. In your Echo Dot settings menu, tap or click on the iHeartRadio option.
2. Once the iHeartRadio screen is showing, tap or click on "Link your account now."
3. You will be taken to the iHeartRadio site. Log in to your account, OR sign up to create a new account. To create a new account, you'll simply enter your email address, a password you want to use, your zip code, year of birth and gender. Make sure to check off the box to agree to the Terms of Service and Privacy Policy as well before you tap the sign up button.
4. Once you have logged into your account or signed up for one and confirmed it, you'll receive a screen saying "Congrats! Your iHeartRadio account is now available on your device."
5. You can now go back to the Amazon Alexa app and go to the iHeartRadio option of your menu to search for or browse radio content.

Note: *Alexa cannot repeat any music played on iHeartRadio. She can, however, skip to another song.*

Tip: *To learn more about what songs your Echo Dot is playing simply ask, "Alexa, who is this?," "Alexa, what album is this?" and "Alexa, what song is this?"*

How to Listen to TuneIn Radio

TuneIn Radio provides both a local and international approach to listening to music, sports, news and entertainment offerings from around the world. You can choose from live global newscasts to international radio stations and specialty podcasts that you cannot get anywhere else. Listen to your favorite local stations digitally or look for radio stations to listen to by musical genres. This is a great free app to enjoy music from your local regions and also music or radio content from around the world!

To listen to TuneIn radio content, you can do several things:

1. Say "Alexa, TuneIn (name of content or program)." The Echo Dot will try to find a matching item from TuneIn based on your spoken request.
2. Go into the Alexa app on your mobile device or the Echo.amazon.com site on a web browser. Tap or click on the TuneIn option on your side menu. You can navigate through the various options for genres or types of programs and then tap or click on the one you want to listen to on Echo Dot. It will begin playing, if available at that time.

How to Listen to Pandora

Echo Dot supports connection with the Pandora music service. Pandora is a streaming internet radio program which offers both free and subscription-based service. With the Pandora website or app, you simply choose an artist or type of music you like and a special radio station is created for you based around this preference featuring similar music to your tastes. You can then access these stations at any time to enjoy a variety of music.

To use a Pandora account with the Echo Dot:

- Open the Alexa app on your mobile device OR open the echo.amazon.com web portal on a compatible web browser.
- On the left side panel, tap or click on "Pandora."
- You should now see "Link a Pandora account to Amazon Echo Dot" (or Echo) along with a blue link, which says "Link your account now." Click on the link.

You will be taken to the Pandora site and given two choices. You can either "Create a Pandora Account" or select "I have a Pandora Account" if you already have one. Tap or click on the appropriate choice here.

If you already have an account, tap or click on "I have a Pandora Account" and then enter your associated email address and password to log in. Once connected, you will have access to all of your stations listed for use in your Alexa app or the Echo web portal.

If you do not have an account, tap or click on "Create a Pandora Account." Creating an account is free. It will require entering your preferred email address, password, and details such as postal/zip code, date of birth and gender. Agree to the terms of service by checking the applicable box and then tap or click on "Create Account Now" button.

If you are creating an account for the first time, you should familiarize yourself with the Pandora website at Pandora.com or via the mobile app for your particular device. You will be able to learn about customizing your stations, any subscription options, and other important features of this streaming music service.

To access Pandora music through your Echo Dot, simply speak a request such as "Alexa, play Kelly Clarkson Pandora." If you've already got a Pandora station based on Kelly Clarkson, Alexa may confirm you are asking to play it. It will start playing music from the station.

If you don't have a Kelly Clarkson Pandora station set up, it will ask if you'd like to create one. After saying "Yes" to this question, Alexa will add the channel to your listing and beginning playing music from the channel. You can simply say "Alexa, stop" at any time during Pandora playback to end the streaming music.

How to Listen to Spotify

The Amazon Echo Dot also supports connection with the Spotify music service. Spotify is a streaming music service free and subscription-based service. With the Spotify program or app, you can search for music by artist, album, song, genre, playlist or record label. You can play available songs and create your own playlists of songs that are available. You can then access the music at any time to enjoy it on your preferred device, including Amazon Echo Dot, but you will need to have a Spotify premium account to do so.

To use your Spotify premium account with the Echo Dot:

1. Open the Alexa app on your mobile device OR open the echo.amazon.com web portal on a compatible web browser.

2. On the left side panel, tap or click on "Spotify."

3. You should now see the Spotify logo, and a "Link your account" blue link. Click on the link to follow the necessary instructions to link Spotify to your Amazon Echo account.

Once you have linked your Spotify premium account, you now have access to any of your available playlists. Simply ask "Alexa, play my hard rock playlist," or whatever playlist you would like to hear and Alexa should begin playing your music. It's also been noted that the Echo Dot supports Spotify connect which will allow seamless hand off of the music you're playing between various devices such as your phone, tablet, computer and Echo Dot.

How to Buy Music

When playing a song that you don't currently own that is part of Amazon's digital music store, you can purchase that track. Alexa may ask after the preview if you'd like to purchase the song, or you can simply say "Alexa, I'd like to buy this song." Your 1-click payment settings will be used to make the purchase and the song you should be added to your Amazon Music library for playback.

Note: *If you have set up a 4-digit passcode to verify your 1-payment purchases, you may also need to speak this to the Echo Dot before your purchase is made.*

Music Controls

You can control music via your spoken requests, or by using some of the Echo Dot's top area controls, or through the Alexa app/Echo web portal.

With Echo Dot's controls:

- Press the + to increase volume.
- Press the − to decrease volume.
- Press the • to interrupt music and speak a request.

With your voice:

You can speak a variety of different requests to control music, including:

- Alexa, play "Song name" by "Artist name" (to play a specific song).

- Alexa, play Prime music (if you are a Prime member it will give you randomly selected music that is free for Prime members to enjoy).
- Alexa, stop (to stop playback).
- Alexa, play next song or Alexa, play previous song.
- Alexa, mute (to mute the sound).
- Alexa, repeat (to repeat previous request or song).
- Alexa, shuffle "playlist name" (to randomly play back from a specific playlist).
- Alexa, turn it up or Alexa turn it down.
- Alexa, play the "station (name)" (to play from iHeartRadio or TuneIn).
- Alexa, TuneIn "program or station (name)" (to play a specific program).

With the Alexa app or site:

You can also use the Alexa app or at your echo.amazon.com account area on a web browser to control music playback.

On the left side of your app or web account area (you may have to click on the three horizontal lines to see it) you can choose from "Now Playing," "Amazon Music," "iHeartRadio" or "TuneIn." Tap on any of these to select from music or audio programs to play back.

Any music you begin playing will show up on the bottom of your app or screen. You will see the name of what you are currently playing, as well as a previous button, play/pause button, next button and to the very right of those a volume icon. Tap or click on any button to adjust that particular aspect of the music or other audio you are playing.

On the Amazon Music controls area, you will also have an icon for shuffle, to shuffle playback of your music and an icon for repeat, to repeat selections. These two icons (as seen in the preceding image) may not appear on the TuneIn or iHeartRadio controls.

Note: *You can also go to your "Home" area of your app, or at echo.amazon.com account on a browser. Here you can scroll through all of your recent requests and music or audio playbacks. You can hover over an album, artist, playlist or station image and should see a play button to begin playing that particular selection.*

Stream Music from iTunes, Spotify, or others using Pairing Tap with Devices

You can use the Echo Dot to play iTunes, Spotify (non-premium membership), Google Play Music or other audio coming from a laptop or mobile device through the Echo Dot. You will basically use the Echo Dot as a wireless Bluetooth speaker.

1. Say "Alexa, Pair Bluetooth" and wait for the voice prompt.
2. Go into your laptop or mobile device's Bluetooth settings and pair with or connect to the Echo-2GJ. This may take several moments.
3. Once it has connected, you can stream sound from your laptop to the Echo Dot as a wireless speaker.
4. You can unpair your laptop or device from the Bluetooth in several ways, such as going back into your device's Bluetooth settings and shutting it off, or by telling the Echo Dot, "Alexa, unpair Bluetooth."

Notes: See the more detailed Spotify section on how to connect a premium Spotify account to your Echo Dot account.

Music streamed to the Dot as a standalone speaker may be significantly lower in volume. Hooking the Dot up to a more robust speaker or stereo system will give a much better experience.

How to Create To Do Lists, Shopping Lists and More

You can make your own lists on the Echo Dot and then access them through your Alexa app on your mobile device, or with your computer's web browser through the Amazon Echo web portal.

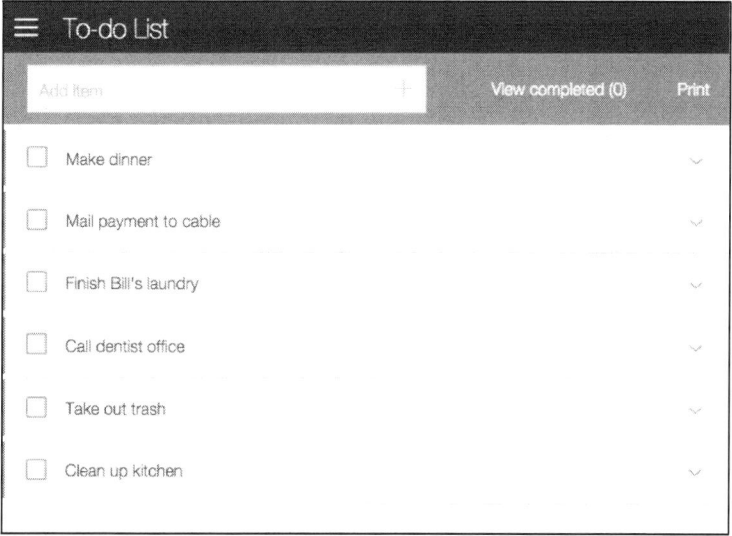

For example, you can create a to do list, a shopping list, or even a goals list to retrieve later on.

To do so simply say "Alexa, add milk to my to do list," or "Alexa, I need to make a birthday cake for Joe." Alexa will store these items on a running list you can access later on in the Alexa app on your mobile device. You can also print out the list for more convenience.

You can also go to the http://echo.amazon.com site and log in with your Amazon account login to see your lists and other Alexa requests.

How to use Echo Dot with Google Calendar

If you have an active Google Account, you can connect your Google Calendar with the Echo Dot to check on various events. If you don't have a Google Calendar, you can create a free account at calendar.google.com.

Once you have your Google Calendar you can connect it to Echo Dot in the Alexa app.

- Go to the "Settings" area of the Alexa app.
- Choose "Calendar," which is listed under Account.
- Link your Google Calendar to the Echo Dot on the next screen.

Once you have linked your Google Calendar, you can ask your Echo Dot (Alexa) various questions such as "Alexa, when is my next event?" or "Alexa, what's on my calendar?" You can even ask the Echo Dot more specifically "Alexa, what's on my calendar for Monday?" and you will receive the latest info, based upon the events you've added to your Google Calendar.

Note: *The Echo Dot will not read events that Google has placed on calendars such as holidays, but will read events you add to your calendar. The Echo Dot can only read back items you have entered onto your Google Calendar. It cannot add items to your calendar at this time.*

To unlink your calendar, complete the following steps:

- From the Alexa app select "Settings."
- Select "Calendar," which is under Account.
- Locate and click on the blue link that reads "Unlink Google Calendar account."

How to use the Skills Features on Echo Dot

The Skills feature offers a variety of different games, services and fun features you can enable to use with the Echo Dot. Examples include a Movie Quote Game, a Magic 8 Ball, a Stock Portfolio Quotes feature and even a feature that allows you to order from Domino's Pizza in your area.

To use a Skills feature:

Open the Alexa app or go to Echo.Amazon.com website and make sure you are logged in with your proper account info.

4. On the left side panel find the word "Skills" and tap or click on it.

5. You'll now see a listing of all the different Skills features you can add the use of to your Echo Dot. To add any Skill feature, all you need to do is tap or click on the "Enable" button to the right of that Skill. It may take several moments.

6. To use that Skill feature on your Echo Dot, simply speak the instructions to Alexa that are needed to

launch the feature. Each Skill's description will tell you that specific command (i.e. "Alexa, start Presidential Trivia" or "Alexa, open Domino's.")

How to order a Pizza or Uber on the Dot

The Skills mentioned in the previous section include specific businesses that you can associate with your Dot, if they apply to your location. For example, both Domino's Pizza and the Uber ride service have Skills you can enable for your Dot.

To order a pizza:

1. Go to the side menu area on your Alexa/Echo app or at the echo.amazon.com web portal.
2. Choose "Skills."
3. Enter "Dominos" in the search bar.
4. Tap or click on the Domino's Pizza skill.
5. Tap or click on the Enable skill button.
6. Make sure you have a Domino's Pizza Profile set up via Dominos.com website. The profile will need to have an Easy Order or a recent order saved for the skill to work.
7. Once you have all of the above, you can say "Alexa, open Dominos" or "Alexa, open Domino's and place my easy order."

To order an Uber ride:

Uber is the ride service that lets customers get a ride and pay for it all through use of a mobile app. You can also use the service with your Dot speaker, if the service is available in your location and you have an Uber account. Here's how to use it on the Dot:

1. Go to the side menu area on your Alexa/Echo app or at the echo.amazon.com web portal.

2. Choose "Skills."
3. Enter "Uber" in the search bar.
4. Tap or click on the Uber skill.
5. Tap or click on the Enable skill button.
6. You will need to have the Uber app or an Uber account linked to the Alexa skill.
7. Once you have all of the above, you can say "Alexa, ask Uber to request a ride" or "Alexa, ask Uber to call me an SUV from my home (or office)" or even "Alexa, ask Uber to change my default location."

Keep in mind that with some Skills on the Echo, Tap and Dot, there are quirks, so it may take a bit of a learning curve to get the specific skills working properly for your situation. In the next section, you'll learn about 10 other skills you may want to try with your Dot.

Ten Cool Skills to Try on Dot

Ask My Buddy – The Ask My Buddy skill provides an extremely helpful service for providing personal alerts. In the instance that someone has fallen or is unable to reach a phone or other device to get help you can use this voice skill. Simple saying, "Alexa, ask My Buddy to alert (name)" or "to alert everyone," will send a notification to those people letting them know you may need assistance. The skill will need some initial setup to program in any individuals you want notified by an alert.

Amazing Word Master Game – By enabling this particular skill, you will have access to a fun game you can play to help stretch your vocabulary. Once enabled, simply say "Alexa, ask Word Master to play a game," or "Alexa, open Word Master" and you'll be part of a game where you must say a word starting with the last letter of the word Alexa says. You can go back and forth with this and earn points for bigger words to tally a high score!

BBC – The BBC skill can provide you with a flash briefing of the latest headline news at your request. Many individuals feel this source gives a good unbiased overall collection of news headlines. Simply enable the skill and say, "Alexa, what's my flash briefing?" or "Alexa, what's in the news?" and you'll get the latest headline news spoken to you.

Crazy Fact – With this skill enabled, you'll be learning things you probably never knew before, and some may even cause a chuckle or two. Use it to impress your friends, family and coworkers with some random, crazy facts! All you need to do is enable the skill and say, "Alexa, start crazy fact," to let the fun begin!

Expedia – If you use the Expedia travel service frequently this is a great skill to have enabled. Once you have it set up and linked to your account online, you can say, "Alexa, open Expedia," and then ask things like, "Alexa, ask Expedia when is my flight?" You can even ask it "Alexa, ask Expedia to reserve a car," for your next trip!

Jeopardy J6 – This is a fun daily game you can enable for your Dot or other Alexa/Echo devices. It provides a new daily set of six clues (Monday through Friday) to which you must speak the correct question. Test your knowledge daily on a variety of topics by saying, "Alexa, let's play Jeopardy!"

The Motley Fool – Got stocks? If you like tracking prices on the stock market of various publicly-traded companies, this is a skill to enable. You can simply say, "Alexa, ask The Fool for Amazon" to get the latest stock quote for a company. The Fool also helps you create a Watchlist of stocks for easier monitoring.

7-Minute Workout – If you're looking to get your physical fitness on, this is the Skill to use. The skill provides you with exactly what the title says, a guided set of instructions for a full workout of seven minutes of different exercises. This is great at your home, or on the go, for example if you're in a hotel room and want to get yourself some quick exercise. Enable the skill and say, "Alexa, start seven-minute workout" to get moving!

The Bartender – This is a really cool skill for anyone who is hosting a get together, dinner, party, or other event and needs help with the drinks situation. With The Bartender skill enabled you can say, "Alexa, ask the bartender, what's in a Bloody Mary" and get the proper ingredients in their right amounts. Not only that, you can say "Alexa, ask the bartender for a drink with orange juice," or any other ingredient you have or even say, "Alexa, ask the bartender to surprise me" and get random drink to test out. It's got over 12,000 recipes to go around!

Thunderstorm Sounds – Depending on where your Dot is located, you may want to enable Thunderstorm Sounds as a skill. This provides you with great background noise which simulates the sounds of storms. It can be useful for creating a relaxing environment to help get to sleep in certain rooms, especially if you take your Dot on trips. Simply say, "Alexa, tell thunderstorm sounds to play," and it will generate the background sounds of a storm!

There are currently hundreds of different skills available through the Echo/Alexa app or web portal. These include different categories across a large range of topics including games, weather, sports, news, business, smart home, utilities, productivity, shopping, music, and more! Simply go to the "Skills" option on the sidebar of the Echo web portal or mobile app and find the best ones for your needs!

Echo Dot Accessories

The Echo Dot interactive speaker does a lot of great things right out of the box. However, it can be further enhanced with all sorts of extra accessories, depending on the owner's needs. Among the items one can purchase to go with the Dot are cables, cases, stands, carrying cases, speakers, and portable power bases.

Protective case – There are special protective cases sold separately from the Dot speaker. These cases are made of leather or fabric in a variety of colors and styles. They not only protect the Dot from potential dust or dirt around it, but also will help it look more stylish in any surroundings. The Amazon website sells cases specific to the Dot in styles such as Charcoal Leather, Merlot Leather, Sandstone Fabric, and Indigo Fabric.

In addition to the cases that Amazon has for the Dot, there are some great third party alternatives. Among them are cases that resemble stylish items for a bookshelf or nightstand such as an owl, skull, or other interesting pieces. Use these to keep your Dot stylishly available and to also have a great conversation piece on display!

3.5 mm audio cable – The Echo is a great mini speaker by itself, but you can also connect a 3.5 mm audio cable. You can use this to connect the Echo Dot to a portable speaker or full-sized stereo system. To do this, you'll need to pick up an optional 3.5 mm audio cable if you don't already have one. This will give the Dot even more robust sound than it already packs in its small size!

Portable carrying case – If you're on the go between different living locations or travel often, you may want to bring your Dot with you. With a portable carrying case, you can pack your Dot inside along with its power cable and brick to make the device easier to transport while also protecting it from harm on the go. These cases generally cost $12 or less and are available in a variety of colors to choose from.

Portable power base – At the time of this original publication, the Amazon Tap was the only of the three interactive speakers that was portable. However, some cool accessories have been developed by third party sellers on Amazon that allow for the Echo or Echo Dot to be portable as well!

With these portable power bases, you can bring your Dot all around the house or elsewhere with ease. Connect your Dot to the power base and then plug the power base into the wall charger and you're good to go!

Bluetooth Speaker – With the addition of a portable Bluetooth speaker, you can really unleash some great sound from the Dot. There are a variety of great models on the market that you can pair up with your Dot and stream music or other audio content to. Many of these speakers cost $100 or less and provide a great enhanced audio experience from the already powerful Dot speaker! Recommended top brands include JBL, Beats, and Bose, but there are many other options out there for Dot owners to choose from.

Smart Home Accessories - Amazon constantly adds new functionality to their Echo or Echo Dot speakers, and it seems as if eventually these devices could really become central devices that can control your entire home. Right now you can use your Echo Dot to control Belkin WeMo, LIFX, TP Link, Phillips Hue, and other compatible Wi-Fi devices.

The Echo Dot allows for connecting to and controlling various home automation devices. With this new feature, you can control your compatible products from these manufacturers by using voice commands to the Echo Dot. These products include select Belkin WeMo and Phillips Hue light products such as the WeMo Switch, Insight Switch and Light Switch, the Phillips Hue A19, Lux, BR30, Bloom and Lightstrip, and Wink. Click here for an entire list of Echo Dot or Echo compatible devices.

Using Dot with Compatible Smart Home Devices

To set this feature up, you must own one or more of the compatible products and have them set up according to the manufacturer's instructions. Some of the brands that provide compatible devices or items include Phillips, TP-Link, LIFX, WeMo, Cree, GE, Leviton, Nest, and Logitech Harmony.

Once any of these compatible devices are set up and part of your home network (requires installation of a compatible mobile app), you can have the Echo Dot discover any of the devices on your home network. Simply say "Alexa, discover my appliances," and the Echo Dot will take about 20 seconds or so to discover your compatible devices.

An alternate method for this is to go into your Alexa app or the Echo.amazon.com website with your log-in and select "Smart Home" from the left side panel menu. You can then choose "Get More Smart Home Skills" to add specific brand apps for your Dot, or you can select "Discover devices" to link up your latest compatible devices to the Dot. Keep in mind that you may be required to set up an account via your specific device's instructions in order to link the device to Alexa.

Now, you should be able to use voice commands to control the items based on its name on your device app or Echo app.

For example, you can say:

- "Alexa, turn on Jim's bedroom light" OR "Alexa, turn off Jim's bedroom light."
- "Alexa, dim kitchen lights to 40 percent" OR "Alexa, turn kitchen lights to 100 percent."
- "Alexa, turn on the coffee maker."
- "Alexa, turn on the outdoor decorations."
- "Alexa, open my garage door."

Creating a Smart Home Group of Devices

You can also create groups in the Alexa/Echo app or web portal to help control multiple smart devices with one spoken command.

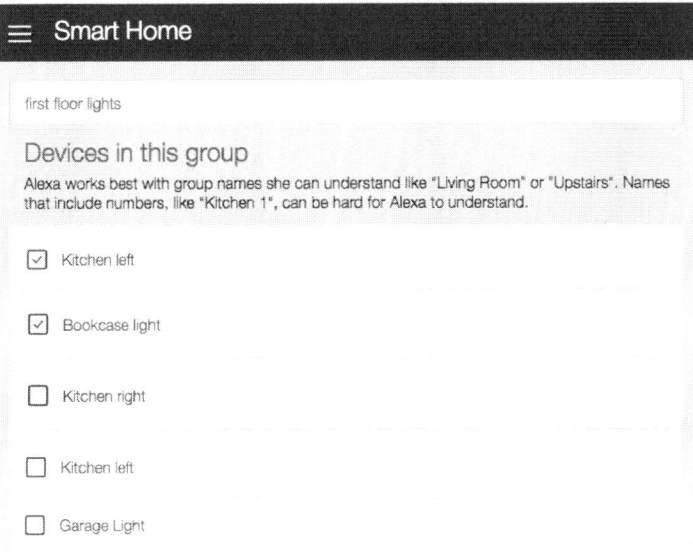

So if you have a number of Smart devices such as multiple Wi-Fi bulbs in a room or on a floor, you might create a group name to be able to control all of those lights with a single voice command.

For example, you may want to create a group called "Living room" and associate all the Wi-Fi bulbs you have in the living room with that group.

Or you might want to create a group such as "First Floor" and put all the lights on the first floor in that group, or even "All lights" or "Whole House" to give control over the entire home full of lights.

To do this, you will need to have already linked (discovered) compatible smart home devices with your Echo.

Here's how to create a group of several smart devices:

1. Choose "Smart Home" from the left side panel of your app or web portal.
2. Next, choose "Create group."
3. Enter a name for your group, such as "First floor" or "Living room."
4. Check off any devices you want associated with the group.
5. Scroll to the bottom of the screen and click or tap on "Save" button.

You should now have a group of devices created and associated with your Echo account. The Echo should now respond to your commands for this group such as "Alexa, turn on living room," or "Alexa, turn off living room."

Quick Tip: Create many different groups to help give different name options for speaking commands to the Alexa. For example, "Lower level lights" and "First floor lights" could be two groups referring to the same set of Wi-Fi lights.

Note: Refer to the included instructions with any of the accessories you purchase along with the Amazon Echo Dot for any connection and troubleshooting issues. If you own an Amazon Echo or Tap and added the Echo Dot onto the same Amazon account in your home, you should be able to use any automation devices you had previously set up for the Echo/Tap.

Some Quick Dot Q&A's

Here are some questions you may have about the Echo Dot. These are the best answers available at the time of this publication in 2016-17.

Do I need an Amazon Echo or Tap to have the Dot?

No, you do not. You can simply use the Dot as your main device if you want. The Echo features a bigger sound as it is a bigger speaker. The Dot has adequate sound for its size and will perform the same general features as its cousins the Echo and Tap.

Do I need an Amazon Prime membership for the Dot to work?

No, you do not need an Amazon Prime membership in order to use the Dot. You will need a free Amazon.com account if you do not already have one. Prime is a great enhancement for the Dot in terms of being able to listen to more music and a few other features, but it is not required for the device to operate.

Can I have a Dot, Echo, and a Tap all together in my home or other area?

Yes, it is possible to have multiple devices in your household or other environment you want to use them in. Each device needs to be set up separately as specified in the app instructions. Also realize, that asking for music to play on one device won't make it play simultaneously on the other devices.

Can I put a Dot in different floors and/or rooms of my home?

Yes, you can use multiple Dots throughout your home, which makes the voice interaction even easier. The Dot in the area you are closest to will usually be able to pick up your voice command. These can help form the basis of a smart home for many households.

Do all Dot devices in my home (or other environment) need to be connected to the same Amazon account?

No. You can choose to hook up each Dot to a separate Amazon account (such as each family member's individual account), or all to the same account.

Can I bring Dot from my home on a trip or to an office, etc.?

Yes, as long as you have your power source and an active Wi-Fi connection at the place you go to, you should be able to connect your Dot through the Alexa/Echo app or website in the new location and use it.

Is the Dot able to be portable in my home or other area, so I can move it around and use it without it being plugged in?

The Dot is required to be plugged into a power source such as a wall socket in order to operate. With that said, there are accessories being sold (as mentioned in the Accessories section) that allow for the Dot to connect to a small power base station that can make it portable. As always, consult the item specifics as well as customer reviews and feedback before purchasing any third party devices for your Dot.

Get Help with Issues or Provide Feedback

You may find that you need additional help with an issue that arises with your Echo Dot device. Luckily, there is an Amazon Echo Dot support team to help respond to your help requests.

The Echo Dot is also likely to get more features and options as new software is released and as third party apps are integrated. It is helpful to provide any suggestions or feedback to Amazon so that they'll know what Echo Dot owners like, dislike or want to see added or changed for the device.

To help provide feedback to or get help from the Amazon Echo Dot support staff:

1. Go into your Alexa app or Echo web portal settings area on the left side.
2. Tap or click on "General Feedback" option.
3. You will be taken to a "What can we help you with?" section.
4. Here you can select an issue to address or type of feedback to give, such as "New Feature Request," "Voice Request," or "Alexa App."
5. Once you've selected the appropriate issue, you can enter your feedback or Echo Dot issue into the box provided.
6. Tap or click on "Send E-mail" to send in your feedback or issue to the support team.

Conclusion

The Amazon Echo Dot is a unique device, and there are surely many new features coming for this little powerhouse in the future as Amazon and 3rd party app developers continue working to provide additional functionality.

The Echo Dot seems like it has the potential to possibly be a whole house coordinator, making a home into a smart home. While this functionality is not yet there, it is easy to imagine the Echo Dot controlling lights, thermostats, TV, and other household items like robotic vacuums. There is big potential here, and hopefully it will be developed as the Echo Dot matures into all it could be.

As it is now, the Echo Dot provides you with a lot of fun along with several useful features. With its high quality speaker, the Echo Dot provides an excellent music playing experience, and it helps you unleash the power of the Prime Music benefit from your Amazon Prime subscription. The list feature makes it easy to keep your grocery and other To Do lists coordinated among all your mobile devices. Any time you have some type of question or argument over something, Alexa is there to help solve the problem if you simply ask.

Because this device is so new, it is imperative for you to stay up to date with the latest on the Echo Dot in order to get the most out of this device and truly unleash its power.

Other guides by Shelby Johnson

Amazon Fire TV User Manual: Guide to Unleash Your Streaming Media Device

Amazon Prime Manual: Music Movies & Lending Library Membership Guide

Apple TV User's Guide: Streaming Media Manual with Tips & Tricks

Facebook for Beginners: Navigating the Social Network

Google Nexus 7 User's Manual: Tablet Guide Book with Tips & Tricks!

How to Get Rid of Cable TV & Save Money: Watch Digital TV & Live Stream Online Media

iPad Mini User's Guide: Simple Tips and Tricks to Unleash the Power of your Tablet!

iPhone 5 (5C & 5S) User's Manual: Tips and Tricks to Unleash the Power of Your Smartphone! (includes iOS 7)

iPhone 6 User's Manual: Tips & Tricks to Unleash the Power of Your Smartphone! (includes iOS 8)

Kindle Fire HDX & HD User's Guide Book: Unleash the Power of Your Tablet!

Kindle Paperwhite User's Manual: Guide to Enjoying your E-reader!

Roku User Manual Guide: Private Channels List, Tips & Tricks

Samsung Galaxy S5 User Manual: Tips & Tricks Guide for Your Phone!

Samsung Galaxy Tab 4 User Manual: Tips & Tricks Guide for Your Tablet!

Printed in Great Britain
by Amazon